Office of the Mayor

Murfreesboro, Tennessee

PROCLAMATION

WHEREAS, the 2016 Pastoral Anniversary Committee along with the members of First Baptist Church Murfreesboro will celebrate Pastor James M. McCarroll, Jr.'s 10th year anniversary; and

WHEREAS, he is a native of Nashville, Tennessee and received a Bachelors of Business Administration Degree from Tennessee State University and also received a Master of Divinity Degree from Colgate Rochester Crozer Divinity School; and

WHEREAS, he was licensed to preach and ordained into the ministry at New Hope Missionary Baptist Church in Nashville, Tennessee and has spread God's word across the United States as well as internationally; and

WHEREAS, in addition to pastoring First Baptist Church Murfreesboro, Reverend McCarroll is the Moderator of the Stones River District Association and oversees the work and fellowship of over 20 churches in the greater Nashville area.

NOW, THEREFORE, I, SHANE MCFARLAND, MAYOR, of the City of **MURFREESBORO, TENNESSEE** on behalf of the entire City Council do hereby proclaim August 27, 2016 as a day to honor

REVEREND JAMES M. MCCARROLL, JR

and urge all citizens to join us in honoring this remarkable man and in celebrating his life as Pastor of First Baptist Church Murfreesboro.

In witness whereof, I have hereunto set my hand and caused the seal of this city to be affixed

Mayor _Shane McFarland_

Date _August 27, 2016_

To the First Baptist Church Family,

"Alone we can do so little, together we can do so much." -Helen Keller

As I reflect on a decade of worship as pastor and congregation, I am truly overwhelmed to think of all that the Lord has done through us. This anniversary is not about me. It is about us. It is a testament to what the Lord can do when we choose to work collaboratively and collectively, let love win, compassion prevail and God's vision override our personal ambitions.

Every day, I stand amazed to lead and serve such an awesome congregation. It has been nothing less than a privilege to walk alongside each of those that have been a part of this congregation since my arrival. You are not only a congregation, YOU ARE MY FAMILY.

To be standing here ten years later full of the joy, peace and love of Christ that emanates from this congregation, it seems almost surreal. Thank you for every act of love and support, every encouraging word and every smile that has inspired me to become the pastor that the Lord Jesus Christ has called me to be. We have seen the Lord do mighty and marvelous things and the best is still yet to come!!!

May the Lord continue to bless and keep this ministry as we move forward for the Kingdom of God and the Gospel of Jesus' sake.

Grateful,

Pastor James McCarroll

The First Baptist Church Family extends its love and appreciation to our pastor, Rev. James M. McCarroll on the occasion of his 10th Anniversary. For ten years, you have been a blessing to us and to this community and we thank you for your service. We honor you as a visionary leader and as a godly man sent to lead us and to be used for God's glory.

Pastor McCarroll, we honor you as a visionary leader sent to lead us. Your vision has forever changed us as we grow in faith and yearn for the knowledge of God. Jesus asked His disciples ".... Are you still sleeping and resting? ...." Matthew 26:45. Your vision has awakened us and given us direction so that we are more aware of the needs of those around us and more focused on rendering service to all aspects of our community. Your vision has given us hope: hope for ourselves; hope for our home and family, hope for our community; and hope for all mankind as a part of God's purposeful plan for our lives.

Pastor McCarroll, we honor you as a godly man who is allowing God to use you for His glory. Thomas Watson, a 17th century English preacher, included the following characteristics in his book *"Picture of A Godly Man"*:

- Man of Knowledge thoroughly trained in religion;
- Man moved by Faith who walks with God;
- Man filled with Love; he Loves the Word and he Loves the Saints;
- Man like God; he has the Spirit of God residing in him;
- Man of Humility, Prayer and Sincerity;
- A Zealous, Patient and Thankful Man;
- A Man that strives to be an instrument for making others Godly.

A man with all these characteristics is rare. We praise God that He sent us a pastor with all of these characteristics, a godly man. In his poem, "What Will Matter" Michael Josephson states that what will matter about your life is "Not what you bought, but what you built; not your success, but your significance; not what you learned, but what you taught; not your competence, but your character. What will matter is every act of integrity, compassion, courage, or sacrifice that enriched, empowered or encouraged others to emulate your example."

We pray, Pastor McCarroll, that you will continue to allow God to use you and that "surely goodness and mercy shall follow (you) all the days of (your) life and (you) will dwell in the house of the Lord for ever." Psalm 23:6

The Church Family

ABOUT THE HONOREE

James Milton McCarroll, Jr. is currently the pastor of First Baptist Church in Murfreesboro, TN.

A Nashville, TN native, he received the Bachelor of Business Administration degree with a concentration in accounting in 1999. He also received a Master of Divinity degree from the Colgate Rochester Crozer Divinity School in 2003.

He is also the Moderator of the Stones River District Association of churches. Through this role, he has been blessed to oversee the work and fellowship of over 20 churches in the greater Nashville area.

He was licensed to preach and ordained to the Christian Ministry at the New Hope Missionary Baptist Church under the late Reverend James C. Turner, Sr. He has since dedicated his life to bringing the message of faith, hope, and love in God through Jesus Christ.

Since his arrival to First Baptist Church in 2006, God has used Pastor McCarroll to bring about a revival in the congregational life to harvest a greater community impact. Led by the power of the Spirit of God, First Baptist Church has witnessed numerical, organizational, and—most importantly—spiritual growth. Inspired by the display of love and unity within the congregation, he has labeled the church as, "the greatest church this side of Heaven." He truly believes that he has only experienced great achievements as a pastor because of the great faithfulness of God and the love and support of the congregation.

Pastor McCarroll has been blessed to teach and preach at numerous venues across the country as well as internationally in Italy, India, Jamaica, St. Thomas, U.S. Virgin Islands, and Guyana. Such venues include conferences, conventions, revivals, and retreats. His desire for those to whom he ministers to experience the fullness of their Christian possibility has caused him to approach ministry with sensitivity toward the holistic need for the faith, hope, and love required to encounter the promises and power that rests within a relationship with God through Jesus Christ. To this end Pastor McCarroll endeavors to impact the world for Jesus Christ through the communication and application of the Word of God.

HE IMPACTS
Pastor James M. McCarroll, Jr.
10

Master and Mistress of Ceremony	Mr. Greg Garrett and Mrs. LaShan Matthews Dixon
Welcome	Minister Pamela Malone Magee *10th Pastoral Anniversary Committee*
Invocation	Minister Chris Williams *Youth Pastor FBC*

DINNER

Starter
garden greens with assorted dressings

Main
CHICKEN BALSAMICO
marinated grilled breast of chicken drizzled with
an aged balsamic reduction served with chef's potatoes,
seasonal vegetables & yeast rolls

Dessert
cheesecake with hershey's chocolate swirled in and
served with raspberry sauce

moist golden carrot cake loaded with freshly grated carrots, pineapple and
walnuts with a touch of cinnamon and nutmeg

water, iced tea & coffee

Music	The Hamilton Brothers Band
Reflections from a Spiritual Father	Pastor H. Bruce Maxwell *Lake Providence Missionary Baptist Church*

HE IMPACTS MEMBERSHIP

Reflections from a Family Member	Elder Robert Allen *Cousin*

HE IMPACTS - MINISTRY

Reflections from a Close Friend	Pastor James C. Turner, III *New Hope Missionary Church*

HE IMPACTS - MISSIONS

Reflections from a Co-Laborer in Ministry	Pastor Vincent Windrow *Olive Branch Church*
Reflections from a Mentor	Dr. T. Scott Swan *Mt. Zion Missionary Baptist Church, Cincinnati, OH*

Special Musical Guest

Closing Remarks
Pastor James M. McCarroll, Jr.

THE PROUST

QUESTIONNAIRE

PASTOR

James McCarroll, Jr.

For ten years, Pastor McCarroll -with his servant heart - has ministered, challenged, and encouraged us to live purposeful God-centered lives. Here he has agreed to undergo a brief, quick and revelatory interrogation to provide a glimpse into the man behind the pulpit.

Which living person do you most admire?
Barack Obama~ to do what he has done it is nothing more than an act of grace.

When and where were you most happiest?
Navarre, Florida 5pm Wednesday October 31, 2013.

What do you consider your greatest achievement?
Pastoring.

What is your most marked characteristic?
My energy.

What do you value most in your friends?
Integrity.

What is your idea of perfect happiness?
A place where there is absolute peace of mind.

What do you consider the most overrated virtue?
Ambition.

What quality do you like most in a man?
Commitment to legacy.

What quality do you like most in a woman?
Selflessness.

What trait to you most deplore in others?
Selfishness.

What trait do you most deplore in yourself?
Procrastination.

Current state of mind?
Grinding.

What is your greatest fear?
Irreversible failure.

If you could change one thing about yourself, what would it be?
To speak 5 different foreign languages.

What historical figure do you most identify with?
FDR (Franklin D. Roosevelt) ~ The way he approached life. FDR had a clear disability but the way he viewed life, the way he viewed his circumstance is that there was never a moment that could not be won. You know the whole there is nothing to fear but fear itself.

What do you consider the lowest depth of misery?
Hopelessness.

What is your most treasured possession?
"My relationship with Christ."

What are your two favorite names?
James and Robyn.

What word or phrase do you most overuse?
"This is for free".

Who are your favorite writers?
Joshua Liebman and Shakespeare.

What is your greatest regret?
Starting late on my dreams.

What talent would you most like to have?
Singing.

What is your favorite motto?
"See it through."

“ What do you
consider the lowest
depth of misery?
Hopelessness

Erin Abernathy
Nonie Bennah
Acesa Brewer
McKinley Corder
Angela Cox
Tamara Crutcher
DeCorey Dalton
Melinda Dalton
Calvin Davis
Ja'Net Davis
Arlene Ezell
Devan Franklin
Annette Gaines-Glimps
Natasha Glover
Rev. Richard Gordon
Lewis Gray
Jackie Jones
Paula Jones
Pamela Malone Magee
Eric Majors
Vivian Miller
Cheryl Mitchell
De'Antwaine Moye
Herb O'Neal
Joshua Person
Jonathan Radford
Danny Sanders
Taylor Seacrest
Marcus Shaw
Geoge Singleton
Joseph Smith
Chris Taylor
Jeanette Taylor-McLin
Brenda Walton
Wayne Walton
Darrell Webb
Chris Williams
Taffiney Williams

The Associate Ministers of
First Baptist Church wish you a
Happy 10th Year Anniversary!

Celebrating a Decade of Ministry
2006-2016

CONGRATS

to Pastor James McCarroll, Jr

for ten years of dedicated service to
First Baptist Church Murfreesboro, TN

Thank you for your service as a Pastor, Evangelist, and Teacher in the local, national and global communities such as Guyana, Italy, India and the Caribbean Islands.

From the McCarroll and Wingfield Family

"How beautiful are the feet of them that preach the gospel of peace and bring glad tidings of good things." -Romans **10:15**

Erin Abernathy
Nonie Bennah
Acesa Brewer
McKinley Corder
Angela Cox
Tamara Crutcher
DeCorey Dalton
Melinda Dalton
Calvin Davis
Ja'Net Davis
Arlene Ezell
Devan Franklin
Annette Gaines-Glimps
Natasha Glover
Rev. Richard Gordon
Lewis Gray
Pamela James
Jackie Jones
Paula Jones
Eric Majors
Vivian Miller
Cheryl Mitchell
De'Antwaine Moye
Herb O'Neal
Joshua Person
Jonathan Radford
Danny Sanders
Taylor Seacrest
Marcus Shaw
Geoge Singleton
Joseph Smith
Chris Taylor
Jeanette Taylor-McLin
Brenda Walton
Wayne Walton
Darrell Webb
Chris Williams
Taffiney Williams

The Associate Ministers of
First Baptist Church wish you a
Happy 10th Year Anniversary!

Celebrating a Decade of Ministry
2006-2016

Congratulations

Pastor McCarroll
on your 10th Pastoral
Anniversary.
It is our most sincere prayer
that God's riches blessings
continue to favor
your ministry.

Now we ask you, brothers, to give recognition to those who labor among you and lead you in the Lord and admonish you, and to regard them very highly in love because of their work. Be at peace among yourselves. ~1Thessalonians 5:12-13

Abernathy, Eric

Black, Carlos

Drake, Jerome

Exum, Demetrius

Gavin, Earnest

Harris, Walter

Herbert, Joe

Hopkins, Craig

Hurd, Ben

Jackson, Charles

Joshua, Farrell

Lyons, Samuel

McAdams, James

McDonald, John

Mclin, Kenneth

Murry, Stan

Pitts, William

Pumphrey, Kenyetta

Risby, Cecil

Roach, Elbert

Rodgers, Clarence

Russell, Warren

Simmons, Jermaine

Slater, Timothy

Tillage, Michael

Vaughan, YT

Walker, Issac

Walker, Jeffrey

Williams, Mount

Winters, Homer

Congratulations
Pastor McCarroll and

Best Wishes
on your 10th Anniversary

We thank you for your faithfulness not only as Pastor of
First Baptist, but as a faithful servant of the Lord.
May God bless and keep you is our prayers.

Vision- This ministry lovingly assists with communion service and assist the female candidates with the baptismal ceremony. As part of caring for this congregation, we visit the sick and those experiencing death or other time of sorrow. Women and girls are empowered to become the Proverbs 31 woman of balanced living by mentoring and providing educational programs, holding evangelistic meetings, and giving bible studies.

Irene Pitts-McDonald - President   Maxine Drake - Vice President   Vanita Sanders - Secretary   Thelma McHenry - Assistant Secretary
Ella Wilkerson* - Treasurer   Gail Williams - Assistant Treasurer   Kathy Alexander* - Chaplain   Florsteen Partee* - Assistant Chaplain
Elma McKnight - Bible Teacher   Saundra Hopkins - Assistant Bible Teacher
Addie Lyons, Ella Frierson*, Eva Woodson, Debra Newman, Gloria Bridgeman, Sharon Fletcher*,
Mae Jackson, Clara Murry, Nancy Vaughan, Heddie Carter, Barbara Winters, Debbie Pumphrey*, Kim Risby
*not pictured

CONGRATULATIONS

2016 USHER MINISTRY

Eric Abernathy
Carlos Black
Natalie Bouie
Wallace Brandon
Cassandra Carson
Heddie Carter
Charita Dozier
Belinda Dublin
Helen Dunnaway
Regina Ellis
Demetrius Exum
Fred Fields
Jackie Fields
Ruby Fletcher
Sharon Fletcher
Raymond Frazier

Zona Frazier
Earnest Garvin
Eric Holiday
Gladys Hiles
Joan Tillage-Hooper
Dorinda Hunter
John Jackson
Jackie Johnson
Wendy Johnson
Monica Jones
Sharon Joshua
Mary Kennedy
Lois Knox
Pamela Lyons
Samuel Lyons
Mary Maupin

Sabrina McCord
Phyliss McDonald
James Miller
Terry Milliner
Frances Mosby
Shelia Nance
Keitha Newman
William Pitts
Debbie Pumphrey
Victoria Richards
Sharon Rodgers
David Roper
Melanie Roper
Teresa Russell
Doris Sanders
Martha Smith

Annie Spann
Douglas Thompson
Gazyola Tillage
McKinley Tuckson
Kim Vaughter
Maggie Vaughn(Honorary)
Marcia Walker
Glenn Wallace
John Washington
Phyliss Whitaker
Ella Wilkerson
Mount Williams
Kerri Woodberry
DeAndra Wright

JUNIORS:
Eric Abernathy Jr.
Tyler Black
Madison Caruthers
Miciah Caruthers
Elijah Darling
Alexandria Hamilton
Asia Lesly
Kenadi Pumphrey
Cory Rodgers
Whitney Russell
Tiara Talley
Jaliah Walker
Jayla Walker
Darra Wright
Di-Anna Wright

Congratulations on your
10th Anniversary

On this special occasion we honor you Pastor McCarroll for your
spiritual leadership and dedication to the members of First Baptist
Church and to the community.

*"And I will give you shepherds after my own heart who will
feed you with knowledge and understanding ~ Jeremiah 3:15*

2016 FBC ARDENT WORKERS

Ann Smith, Barbara Alexander, Bobbie Black, Clara Meels, Corine Scales
Ella Wilkerson, Frances Mosby, Gloria Bridgemn, Irene Pitts-McDonald, Lois Malone,
Ella Frierson, Nancy Vaughn, Saundra Hopkins, Melbra Simmons, Arlene Collins

Congratulations on your 10th Pastoral Anniversary Pastor McCarroll

We Thank God for you and your 10 years of servant leadership to First Baptist Church.

KITCHEN MINISTRY

Alphonse Carter, Heddie Carter, Alfonso Drake, Demetrius Exum, Fred Fields, Jackie Fields, David Hill, Eric Holiday, Alice Hurd, Ben Hurd, Mae Jackson, Dwight Johnson, Monica Jones , Pierre Lyons, Valeria Lyons, Sabrina McCord, Thelma McHenry, Marcus McNeil, James Miller, Terry Milliner, Clara Mills, Francis Mosby, Dominique Murphy, Houston Murphy, Elbert Roach, Doris Sanders, Demus Stewart, Tawanna Story, Gayzolo Tillage, Barbara Tuckson, McKinley Tuckson, Kim Vaughter, John Washington, Mount Williams

We recall, in the presence of our God and Father, your work of faith, labor of love, and endurance of hope in our Lord Jesus Christ ~ 1Thessalonians 1:3

1ST ROW(KNEELING) LEFT TO RIGHT: Kendra Dickerson, Anisha Paul, Brandi Simmons, Jermaine Simmons
2ND ROW LEFT TO RIGHT: Cenetra Davis, Mia Zellers , Brittany Montgomery . **3 ROW LEFT TO RIGHT:** Mike Barker, Renee Barker, Kim Williams, Chris Williams, Tamesha Hudson, LaToya Beard, Anitra Harris, Antwan Buchannan

Congratulations on your 10th year anniversary at First Baptist Church. We thank you for all your guidance and support over the years. We are blessed to have you as our pastor, leader and shepherd.

Love the FBC Youth Department.

First Baptist Church
BIBLE IN 1 YEAR MINISTRY

-WE-
Appreciate
YOU PASTOR MCCARROLL

Addie Lyons, Ruby Rucker Fletcher, Doris Sanders, Walter Phillips, Joe Robinson, Helen Dunnaway, Lois Malone, Ann Smith, Vicky Harris, Phillip McDonald, McKinley Tuckson, Melba Simmons, John Washington, Deborah Newman

CONGRATULATIONS

Thank you for your leadership at First Baptist Church. We give thanks each day that you have been called into ministry with us. We watch as you lead and teach us in so many ways each week, listening to us, celebrating with us, mourning our losses, being present in so many ways in our lives. Thank you for being our Pastor.

With Love,
First Baptist Music Ministry

"Make a joyful noise unto the Lord, all ye lands. Serve the Lord with gladness: come before his presence with singing. Know ye that the Lord he is God: it is he that hath made us, and not we ourselves; we are his people, and the sheep of his pasture. Enter into his gates with thanksgiving, and into his courts with praise: be thankful unto him, and bless his name. For the Lord is good; his mercy is everlasting; and his truth endureth to all generations." ~Psalm 100

CONGRATULATIONS

Pastor James McCarroll
on 10 years of service to our community.
We thank God for your vision and passion
that help to start A City of Grace.
We look forward to what God has in store
for the years to come!

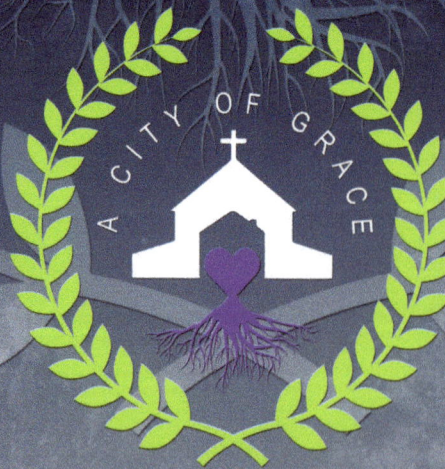

MISSION
TO ENHANCE LIVES BY PROVIDING EDUCATION, HEALTH AND ECONOMIC RESOURCES

ERIC MURRY
Executive Director

DE'ANTWAINE MOYE
Chairman

BOBBIE PORTER
Vice Chairman

PAULA JONES
Secretary

MARITA RICE
Treasurer

DENISE COLE
Governance Chair

MEISHA WALLER
Programming Chair

KATHY FERRELL
Development Chair

BOBBY SMITH

JAMES MCCARROLL

DR. GLORIA BONNER

RON WASHINGTON

A CITY OF GRACE
Community Development Corporation

738 East Castle Street
Murfreesboro, TN 37130
T 615 893 5322 F 615 893 4391

Pastor Vincent L. Windrow

OLIVE BRANCH
CHURCH
Believe · Belong · Become

Congratulations
PASTOR JAMES McCARROLL

Murfreesboro Location
1115 Minerva Drive
Murfreesboro, TN

Service Times:
7:30 am and 12:45 pm

Nashville Location
(Temporary)
800 Youngs Lane
Nashville, TN

Service Time:
9:00 am

Phone: 615-941-1268
E-mail: connect@olivebranchchurch.org
Web: www.olivebranchchurch.org
@OliveBranchTN

Believe.   Belong.   Become.

We are a vibrant community that emphasizes enrichment, excellence, and fellowship through
Outreach, Small Groups, and Impactful Worship! We cannot wait to welcome you to OBC.

DR. A.L. CHAPMAN MINISTRIES
PASTOR | PROFESSOR | AUTHOR | HOMILETICS COACH

AWAKENING
THE PREACHER WITHIN

FOLLOW US ON FACEBOOK | TWITTER | INSTAGRAM | YOUTUBE

HTTP://DRLCHAPMANMINISTRIES.WEEBLY.COM
PHONE | 248.707.4449

CONGRATULATIONS

Pastor James McCarroll on

TEN YEARS OF
TRIUMPH, TENACITY, AND TRANSFORMATION

We are no longer the same because
of our ineffable encounter with you!

BE BLESSED

PASTOR JAMES McCARROLL

10TH ANNIVERSARY CELEBRATION

GREETINGS FROM "THE MOUNT"

Obey your leaders and submit to them, for they are keeping watch over your souls, as those who will have o give an account. Let them do this with joy and not with groaning, for that would be of no advantage to you.

-Hebrews 13:17

MT. ZION
MISSIONARY BAPTIST CHURCH
Jerry D. Marable, Senior Pastor

228 North Maple Street · M'boro, TN 37130 · (615) 893-2080 · mtzionmurf@bellsouth.net or www.mtzionmaple.com

Congratulations!

PASTOR JAMES M. MCCARROLL, JR.
on your 10th Pastoral Anniversary.

"Restoring Hope, One Heart At A Time"

AGAPE PERFECTING PRAISE & WORSHIP CENTER
Pastor Sharon Riley

| IMPACT WORSHIP | SUN 9AM | MORNING WORSHIP | SUN 11AM |
| BIBLE STUDY | WED 7PM | | |

320 SOUTH IVEY LANE
ORLANDO, FL 32811
P: 407.293.6264 | F: 407.293.2966

f Official Agape Perfecting Praise &
Worship Center
& Sharon Y. Riley Ministries

You Tube SharonYRileyMi

Happy 10th Anniversary

Pastor James M. McCarroll, Jr.

**from Pastor & Lady Scovens
and the GMBC Family**

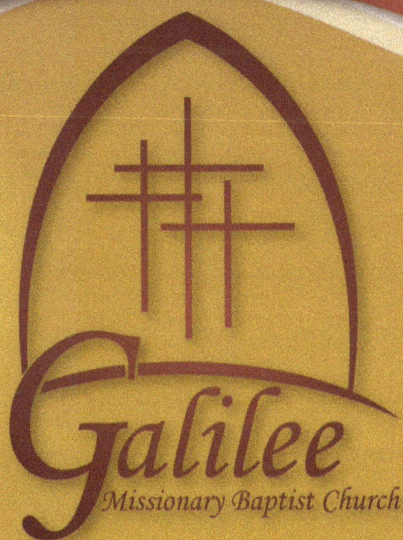

Galilee
Missionary Baptist Church

4129 Northampton Drive
Winston-Salem, NC 27105 • 336.724.3857

Reverend Dr. Nathan E. Scovens, Pastor

www.galileemissionarybaptist.org

Congratulations To
Pastor James McCarroll, Jr.
FIRST BAPTIST CHURCH
10th Pastoral Anniversary

APOSTLE AMOS & YOLANDA HOWARD

LIVING TRUTH
CHRISTIAN CENTER
Partners for Life

ONE CHURCH ~ TWO LOCATIONS
CORPORATE HEADQUARTERS
102 RIDLEY STREET | SMYRNA, TENNESSEE 37167
PHONE: (615) 459-9017 | FAX: (615) 459-8670
WWW.LIVINGTRUTHCC.ORG
FACEBOOK.COM/AMOSLHOWARDMINISTRIES
PERISCOPE.TV/APOSTLE_HOWARD

WORSHIP
SUNDAY - 8:00 AM & 10:00 AM
WEDNESDAY - 7:00 PM

SMYRNA, TN

GADSDEN, AL

Blessed Beginnings
Comprehensive Learning Center
"Empowering Our Children For Success"
State Licensed ♦ 3-Star Facility
Hours of Operation: Monday - Friday 6:00 AM - 6:00 PM
Serving Ages 6 weeks - 4 years | ABEKA Christian Curriculum
615-459-0591 | www.blessedbeginningsclc.org

Give me wisdom and knowledge, that I may lead this people, for who is able to govern this great people of yours? - 2 Chronicles 1:10

HOLY
BIBLE

Congratulations

Pastor James McCarroll
on your
10th Year Pastoral Anniversary

*May God continue to bless you and your ministry
as you continue preaching and teaching His Word!*

Greater First Baptist Church

512 Sixth Avenue North
Lewisburg, TN 37091
Reverend William Herbert Johnson, Pastor

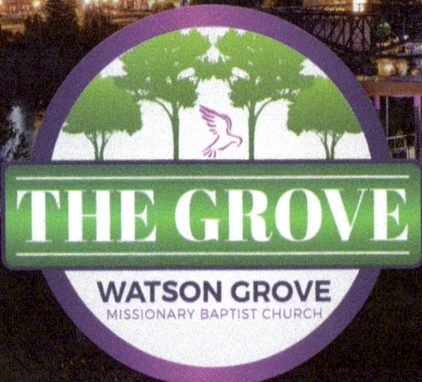

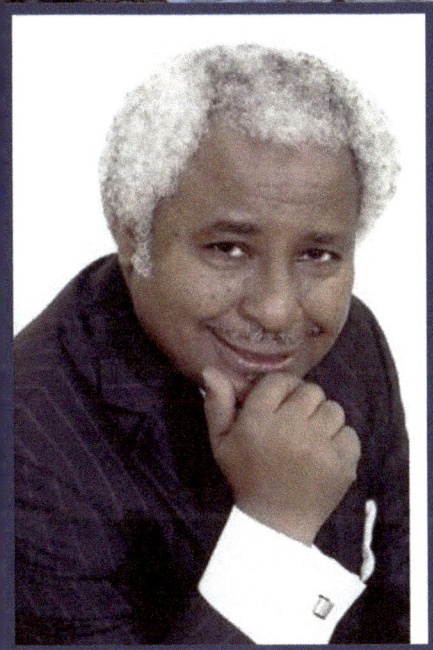

MANUEL SCOTT JR.
Evangelist Author Lecturer

Pastor Mac,
Oceanic Blessings on you
on your glorious
10th Pastoral Anniversary!
Your Friend,
Evangelist Manuel Scott, Jr.

MANUEL SCOTT JR MINISTRIES, INC.
P.O. BOX 8865, LOS ANGELES, CA 90008 U.S.A. (626) 369-6360 MANUELSCOTTJR@YAHOO.COM

Congratulations

to

Pastor James M. McCarroll, Jr.
and
The First Baptist Church Family
on your
10th Pastoral Anniversary

New Pleasant Grove
Missionary Baptist Church

3221 Bain Street, Houston, TX 77026

Rev. Dr. Charles E. Turner, Pastor

713-672-7419 (Office) | 713-672-8191 (Fax)
email: contactus@npghouston.org

www.npghouston.org

CHERRY GROVE
MISSIONARY BAPTIST CHURCH

Congratulations!

PASTOR
JAMES M. MCCARROLL, JR.
FIRST BAPTIST CHURCH

10 years of dedicated
service to God!

Pastor McCarroll,

"On behalf of First Lady Janice Ward
and Cherry Grove churh family,
may God bless you for the time you give,
the work you do, and the care you offer."

Pastor James Ward

God, in His wisdom..
Has gifted you and called you...
In this time...This place..To care for His People.

You do a Wonderful Job!

"Watch, stand fast in the faith, be brave, be strong. Let all that you do be done in love."
~2 Corithians 16:13-14

CONGRATULATIONS
Pastor James M. McCarroll, Jr

Reverend Eric D. Williams and
The Greater Pleasant View Baptist Church
congratulate you for ten years of
Faithful and Faith-filled service.

2710 HILLSBORO RD., BRENTWOOD, TN 37027   I   P 615.373.8219

Reverend Eric D. Williams

*But it must not be like that among you. On
the contrary, whoever is greatest among
you must become like the youngest, and
whoever leads, like the one serving.*
~Luke 22:26

CONGRATULATIONS
Pastor James M. McCarroll, Jr.
on celebrating your
10th Pastoral Anniversary!

Thank you so much for your continuous support of
The American Legion Buster Bedford Post #177
by helping us uphold our four pillars.

AMERICAN LEGION POST #177
BUSTER BEDFORD

The Four Pillars of Service

VETERAN AFFAIRS • NATIONAL SECURITY • CHILDREN & YOUTH • AMERICANISM

MIDDLE TENNESSEE

STATE UNIVERSITY.
COMMUNITY ENGAGEMENT COUNCIL

We are grateful for your leadership and impact throughout the greater community.

Tom Clark, Agent
State Farm Insurance

Lanny Goodwin, Executive Director
Murfreesboro Parks and Recreation

Steve Odom, Pastor
Central Christian Church

Rita C. Shacklett, Director
Linebaugh Public Library System

Judy Smith, Retired Associate Dean of Students
Middle Tennessee State University

Marisela Tapia, ELL Family Liaison
Murfreesboro City Schools

Mary Wade, Retired Board Chair
Murfreesboro City Schools

Paul Latture, President
Rutherford County Chamber of Commerce

Phyllis Qualls-Brooks, Executive Director
Tennessee Economic Council on Women

Eugene Ray, Mayor
Bedford County Government

Bobby Sands, Judge
Maury County General Sessions Court

Joyce Taylor, Social Events Photographer
Daily News Journal/Murfreesboro Magazine

Don Witherspoon, President
MTSU Alumni Association Board of Directors

Derek Blake, Chief Operating Officer
Boys and Girls Club of Middle Tennessee

Jim Crumley, Assistant City Manag
City of Murfreesbo

Harry Gill, City Manag
City of Smyrr

Kathleen Herzog, Executive Direct
Main Street of Murfreesboro and Rutherford Coun

James McCarroll, Pastor and Communi
Engagement Council Cha
First Baptist Churc

Martha Tolbert, Vice President of Finan
Saint Thomas Rutherford Hospit

Scott Walker, Vice Presider
WGNS Rad

Phyllis Washington, Retired Superviso
Rutherford County Schoo

Phillip J. Barnett, Retired Captai
Medical Service Cor
United States Nav

John Hood, Former State Representative and Direct
MTSU University Government Relatior

Rosemary Owens, Coordinato
MTSU University Strategic Partnership

Gloria L. Bonner, Assistant to be Presider
MTSU University Community Relatior

"And I will give you pastors according to mine heart, which shall feed you with knowledge and understanding." ~ Jeremiah 3:15

Saint Thomas Rutherford Hospital Wishes To

THANK YOU

Rev. James M. McCarroll, Jr.

for your service to our community

✝ Saint Thomas
RUTHERFORD HOSPITAL

WEE CARE

510 S. HANCOCK STREET, MURFREESBORO, TN 37130 | P (615) 890-4317

CONGRATULATIONS

With deep appreciation we congratulate
and we thank you, Pastor McCarroll,
for your years of service to the Lord.
Thank you for your unwavering support of the
children and parents at Wee Care Day Care.
Respectfully-

WEE CARE BOARD MEMBERS

Patricia Gaiser
Katie Wilson
Diane Patterson
Mary Glass

Benny Windom
Chris Lilly
Linda Hardymon
Florence Smith

Dana Barrett
Linda Jordan
Jeran Moore
Rochelle Anderson- Director

Congratulations to
Pastor James McCarroll on

10
Years
of wonderful service!

From your friends at

JUST LOVE
COFFEE & EATERY

Murfreesboro West

2863 Old Fort Pkwy, Murfreesboro, TN 37128 • (615) 900-3324 • justlovecoffee.com

Congratulations

Pastor

James M. McCarroll

on your

10th Anniversary Celebration

from

Deacon YT Vaughan

& Family

Congratulations
Pastor McCarroll

10

YEARS SERVICE
AS THE
SHEPHERD

Thank you for always giving me
direction and support

Millicent F. Nelson

First Baptist Church Family

Congratulation Pastor James M. McCarroll, Jr. on your
10th Pastoral Anniversary

THE RABB FAMILY
Mr. Michael Rabb
Dr. Kerri Woodberry Rabb
Mikaela, Kaitlyn and Courtney Rabb

DR. KERRI M. WOODBERRY
The Macourlyn Center for Plastic Surgery

1370 Gateway Blvd Suite 21
Murfreesboro, Tn 3712
Phone: 615-895-910

Congratulations

Pastor James McCarroll
on your 10th Year Annivesary!!!!

Now we "gonna give you this for free". You have blessed our family more than you will ever know. My wife and I say that you have a spiritual wisdom way beyond your chronological years. May GOD continue to use you to touch and bless the lives around you. From your close relatives and friends, to this church and its members, to this community we are very privileged to have you as our shepherd. We pray "El Shaddai" with his almighty power, provide you with the necessary energy, time, health, peace, joy, and happiness to continue many many more years here at First Baptist Church of Murfreesboro.

Once again, congratulations from the

Johnson Family

Derek, LaToya, Derek II, Derryan, Madison C., Miciah C, and Dorothy

Congratulations

Pastor James M. McCarroll, Jr.
on your 10 Year Anniversary
of pastoring
First Baptist Church, Murfreesboro, TN

Murfreesboro Lodge # 12 , Murfreesboro, Tennessee

Left to Right: Bro. Antonio Neely, PM Roy Jordan, WM David M. Sellers, PM Darrel Martin, Bro. Kevin Murry, PM Y.T. Vaughn

2015-2016 OFFICERS

Worshipful Master- David M. Sellers; Senior Warden- Renee Shaw; Junior Warden- Kevin Murry; Secretary- Antonio Neely; Treasurer- Jeff Pearson; Senior Deacon- Patrick Rhodes; Junior Deacon-John Anderson; Senior Stewart- Percy Ford; Junior Stewart-Robert Wilson; Chaplain-Jordan Slay; Marshal- Darrel Martin; Tyler- Y.T. Vaughn

CONGRATULATIONS

To Pastor James M. McCarroll
as we celebrate your
10th Pastoral Anniversary

Bro. John McDonald
Secretary

Bro. Emmitt Quarles
Junior Warden

Bro. Michael Tillage
Worshipful Master

Bro. Marvin Stubbs
Senior Warden

Bro. Glenn Wallace
Treasurer

Bro. Derrick Brown
Senior Deacon

Bro. Douglas Thompson
Junior Deacon

Bro. Dennis Freeney
Chaplain

Bro. James Knight

Bro Kelvin Jones

Bro. Richard Simmons
Senior Steward

S.M. Strayhorne Masonic Lodge No. 347

BROTHER MCCARROLL

on behalf of the
Omicron Sigma Lambda Chapter
of
Alpha Phi Alpha Fraternity, Inc.,

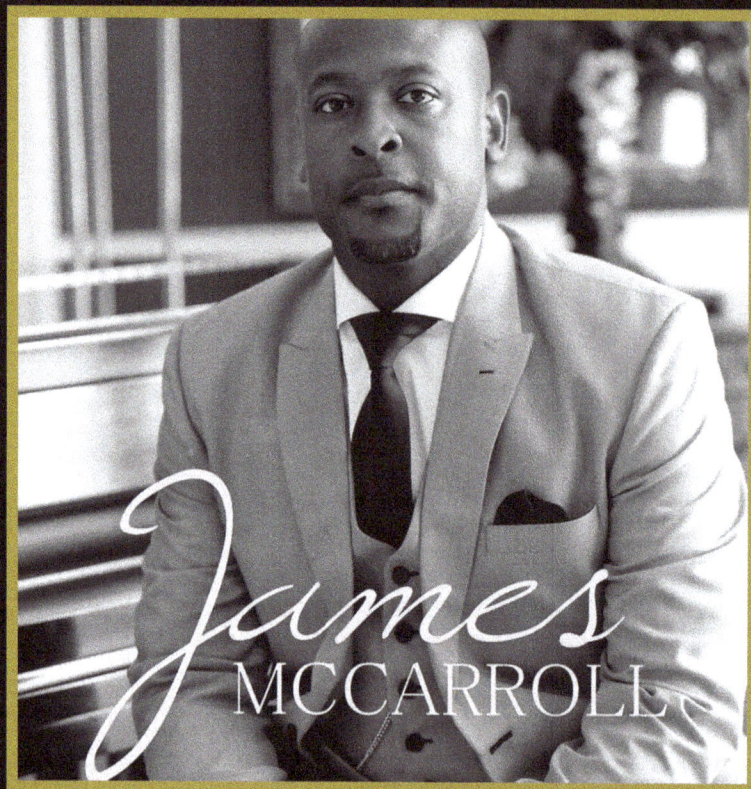

James
MCCARROLL

we congratulate you on 10 years of
service to our church and community!

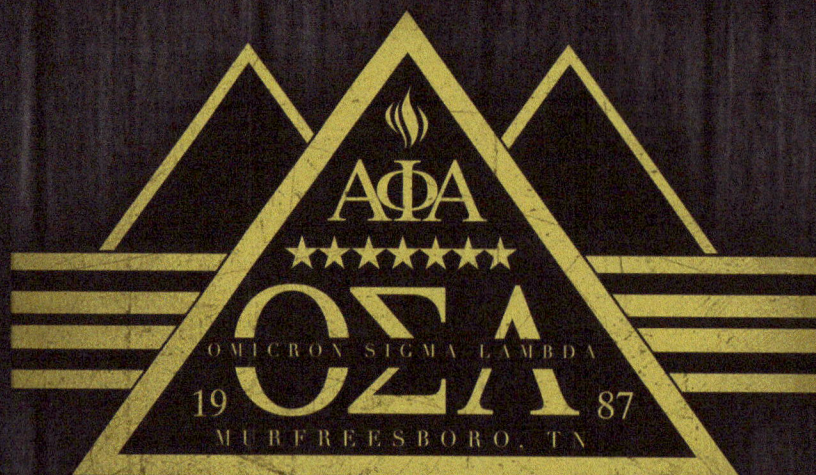

Congratulations
PASTOR MCCARROLL

from the ladies of

Alpha Kappa Alpha
SORORITY, INCORPORATED
Pi Nu Omega Chapter

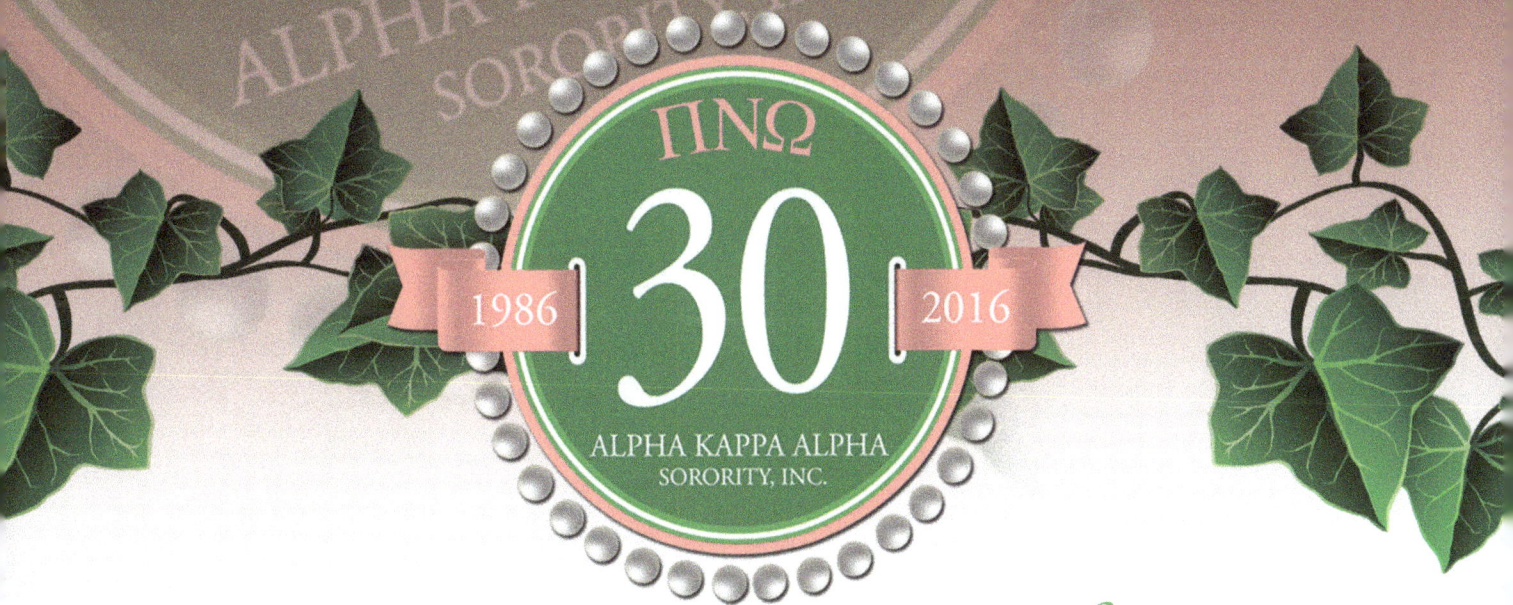

ΠΝΩ

1986 **30** 2016

ALPHA KAPPA ALPHA
SORORITY, INC.

Pi Nu Omega Chapter
Celebrating 30 Years of Service in Murfreesboro, TN

Happy 10th Anniversary
Pastor James McCarroll

A true
Bridge Builder
in our Community.

From the GREAT Men of
OMEGA PSI PHI
FRATERNITY, INC.

Joe Herbert Dr.   Derek Johnson   Jeff Walker
Edward Morant   Sean Adams   Dale Strickland

The Rutherford County Alumnae Chapter of Delta Sigma Theta Sorority, Inc.

Congratulates

Pastor McCarroll

On *10 years* of Pastoral Service

The Lord bless thee, and keep thee;
The Lord makes his face shine upon thee,
And be gracious unto thee;
The Lord give thee peace.

NUMBERS 6:24

Grandma Anna and Me 1853

Nancy L. B. Vaughan

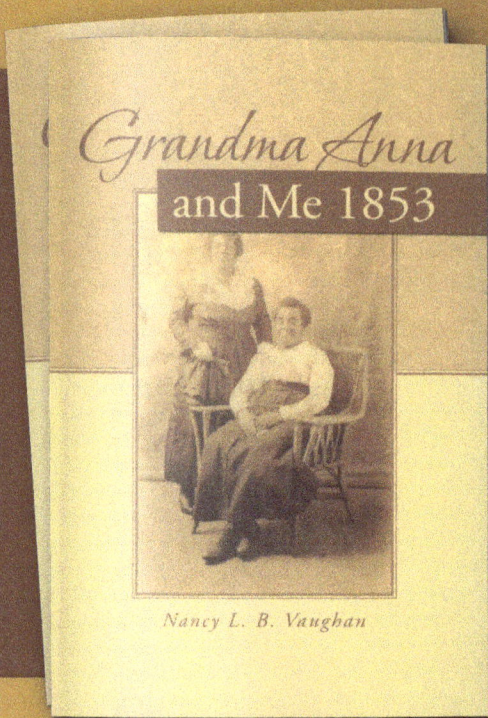

Congratulations
Pastor
James M. McCarroll Jr.
on your
10th Anniversary
Celebration.

"Grandma Anna and Me 1853"
Nancy L.B. Vaughn- Author
(615)895-5532
Book can be purchased at amazon.com.

This simply written, thoughtful, inspiring book "Grandma Anna and Me 1853" through a series of unforgettable short stories and activities allows the reader to reflect on how the power of love and faith, with time and prayer, can change unbearable situations into healthy, satisfying, and successful outcomes. With insight generously laced with humor, Nancy L. B. Vaughan weaves a story of the survival and perseverance of a people.

Congratulations to Pastor James McCarroll

"The NACCP fights for your civil rights"

NAACP
FOUNDED
1909

NATIONAL ASSOCIATION FOR THE ADVANCEMENT OF COLORED PEOPLE

on your 10th Pastoral Anniversary

Murfreesboro Branch of the NAACP
Katie Wilson, President | P (615) 556-7189

CONGRATULATIONS

Pastor
James M. McCarroll, Jr.
on your

10 YEAR
anniversary

Walnut Grove Missionary Church

R.W. Sibert, Pastor
2480 Twin Oaks Dr
Murfreesboro, TN 37130

*Praise God for
Pastor McCarroll
and his
10th Anniversary!*

Pastor Noel Schoonmaker
First Baptist Church
E. Main Street, Murfreesboro TN

Congratulations
&
Best Wishes
on your
10th Pastoral Anniversary!

ST. JOHN MISSIONARY BAPTIST CHURCH
Reverend Charles Lomax, Jr., Pastor

178 Bessie Harvey Avenue
Alcoa, TN 37701
865.982.8021

Pastor James M. McCarroll, Jr.

Wishing you the best Pastoral Appreciation

From
Bishop Calvin C. Barlow, Jr. & Lady Rutha L. Barlow

SANTUARY OF PRAISE
SMBC
SECOND MISSIONARY BAPTIST CHURCH

1000 Halcyon Ave, Nashville, Tennessee 37204 | Phone (615) 298-1832

CONGRATULATIONS
Pastor McCarroll!

Congratulations to you on reaching this amazing milestone of 10 years of pastoral leadership at First Baptist Church! You have been a blessing to my family, and I am so grateful that God led us to this awesome church. May God continue to favor you and bless you, as you courageously and relentlessly pursue Him! The best is yet to come!

Paula & Evan

1Samuel 17 | Matthew 6:33 | 1Thessalonians 5:24

WE THANK GOD FOR YOU

An Appreciation

Pastor James M. McCarroll, Jr.

We appreciate your commitment to the young people in our city and around the state.

Sister Martha Smith & Family
Her great grandsons-
Mason Rowers and Terrance Odom, Jr
(sons of Brittany Rivers and Lindsay Odom)

First Baptist Church Family

An Appreciation

Happy 10th Anniversary
Pastor James McCarroll

From The Russell's
Warren, Teresa, Joshalyn, Whitney and Alex

The Russell Group, LLC | WTR Capital, LLC

First Baptist Church Family

An Appreciation

Pastor McCarroll, thank you for being such a great shepard.
We pray God's abundant blessings and continued strength for you.

CONGRATULATIONS!

Jermaine, Brandi, & Maleah
-SIMMONS-

First Baptist Church Family

An Appreciation

CONGRATULATIONS TO YOU
on your 10th Pastoral Anniversary.
Thank you for the spiritual
IMPACT
you have made in our church and
in our community. My prayer is
that you will continue to be
fruitful in doing the work that God
has called you to do. May He
forever bless and keep you.

-Mary E. Maupin-

First Baptist Church Family

An Appreciation

With cherished memories of
Mrs. Evelyn Anderson Wade
our family esteems you Pastor James McCarroll for
diligently and consistently serving our communities

1 Corinthians 15:58 NIV
Therefore, my dear brothers, stand firm. Let nothing move you. Always give yourselves
fully to the work of the Lord, because you know that your labor in the Lord is not in vain.

1 Timothy 5:17-18 NIV
The elders who direct the affairs of the church well are worthy of double honor, especially
those whose work is preaching and teaching. For the scripture says, "Do not muzzle the
ox while it is treading out the grain," and "The worker deserves his wages."

First Baptist Church Family

An Appreciation

Congratulations on 10 years!

from
Glenn & Lynn Wallace

First Baptist Church Family

In Appreciation

We are happy to congratulate you, Pastor McCarroll, on your 10th year anniversary at First Baptist Church. We pray God continues to bless you in all your endeavors.

With Love
Williams Family
Chris, Kim & Shania

First Baptist Church Family

In Appreciation

Rejoice In The Lord Pastor
For Ten Blessed Years!
We Pray That He Continues
To Keep You
With More Vision To
Come....Love You

CHERRY ARMOR &
EDDIE BROWN

First Baptist Church Family

In Appreciation

We offer a heartfelt
congratulations to Pastor
James McCarroll. We
THANK YOU
for outstanding and
Godly leadership.

Deacon Craig Hopkins, Mother Saundra Hopkins,
Deacon Cecil Risby, Mother Kim Risby and
Alexander Tate

First Baptist Church Family

New Hope Missionary Baptist Church

Congratulates
Pastor James McCarroll for

10
YEARS

of
Pastoral Services to
First Baptist Church Murfreesboro

REV. JAMES TURNER II,
PASTOR

WE CELEBRATE YOU!!

In Appreciation

Congratulations!
Clara Meels & Family

First Baptist Church Family